The Spanish Exploration of South America

EXPLORATION AND DISCOVERY

EXPLORATION AND DISCOVERY

The Spanish Exploration of South America

How the discoveries of Christopher Columbus
and Amerigo Vespucci and the conquests of
Vasco Núñez de Balboa, Francisco Pizarro, and
Pedro de Valdivia created an empire for Spain

Mark McKain

Mason Crest Publishers
Philadelphia

Mason Crest Publishers
370 Reed Road
Broomall PA 19008

Mason Crest Publishers' world wide web address is
www.masoncrest.com

First printing

1 3 5 7 9 8 6 4 2

Library of Congress Cataloging-in-Publication Data
on file at the Library of Congress

ISBN 1-59084-047-X

EXPLORATION AND DISCOVERY

Contents

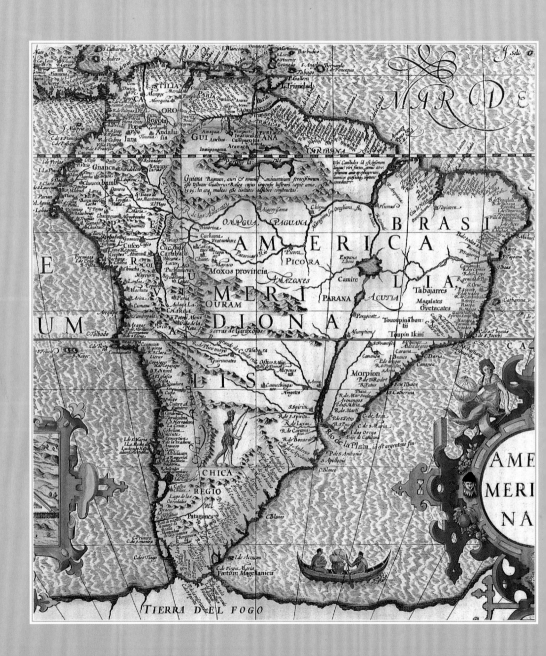

The enormous continent of South America blocked Christopher Columbus's way west to the Far East—his ultimate goal. Spanish explorers soon realized that there were great opportunities to find glory and riches in this "New World."

Discovery of a New Continent

ALMOST EVERY young student knows that Christopher Columbus sailed across the ocean from Spain in 1492, landing in what he called the New World. What some students may not know, however, is that on that voyage Columbus found some islands off the coast of North America. Columbus made a total of four voyages across the Atlantic Ocean. On his third, in 1498, he landed on the mainland of South America.

Columbus was not the only European to see South America around this time. In 1500 a Portuguese explorer named Pedro Cabral was trying to sail around Africa. His ship was blown far to the southwest during a storm. Cabral

Though students have learned that Christopher Columbus discovered the New World in 1492, he did not actually set foot on the mainland of the American continents until 1498. During his third voyage across the Atlantic, Columbus landed on the coast of what is now Venezuela, in South America. Although Columbus still believed that he was in the Indies, he thought this beautiful land might contain the Biblical Garden of Eden.

spotted the eastern coastline of what today is Brazil. However, with Columbus's landing in South America, the Spanish exploration of this continent began.

Ferdinand and Isabella, the King and Queen of Spain, sent Columbus on his third voyage in 1498. Columbus still dreamed of finding a shortcut to Asia. This would allow a trade route to be established between Spain and the countries of the Far East. Today, we buy our *spices* at the grocery store, but in the 15th century, spices were hard to get in Europe. They were as valuable as gold. Furthermore, the Spanish had already lost much of the spice trade to Portugal. The Portuguese had found a route to India and the Spice Islands by sailing east around the tip of Africa. Columbus believed that by sailing west instead, he would reach India and the Spice Islands quicker. Despite the many discoveries of his earlier two voyages, Columbus had not found the gold and spices he had promised the King and Queen.

It was a long, difficult voyage across the Atlantic. Finally, after two months, Columbus sighted land. This was the island of Trinidad off the Venezuelan coast of South

In order to make money, Columbus began capturing the natives of the islands and selling them as slaves. This was against Queen Isabella's wishes. She wanted to make these people into Christians, not slaves.

America. While his ships anchored there, a canoe with 25 natives approached. Columbus tried to talk to them, but they would not come aboard. Admiral Columbus had his men perform a dance to welcome the Indians. But either they didn't like the Spaniards' dancing, or they thought it was a war dance. They showered the sailors with a hail of arrows. Columbus immediately commanded his men to stop dancing and start firing. The Indians rowed away, never to be seen again. Misunderstandings like these would happen again and again as European and native peoples came in contact with one another. Sometimes the encounters would be friendly, but often they would turn violent.

Columbus then sailed to what he thought was another island. There he entered the mouth of a large river. It turned out to be one of the largest rivers in South America—the Orinoco. Columbus knew that such a huge river could not flow from a small island. He wrote in his **log**, "I believe this land may be a great continent that has remained unknown to this day." Columbus felt certain he had at last found his way to Asia.

The American continents are sometimes referred to as the New World. However, these lands were new only to the Spanish, not to the natives who had lived there for thousands of years.

Here, Columbus was more successful in talking with the

King Ferdinand and Queen Isabella of Spain sponsored Christopher Columbus's voyages across the Atlantic. After landing in South America during his third voyage, Columbus wrote to the rulers, "your Highnesses have become the masters of another world."

natives. He was welcomed with great feasts by the *cacique*, or chief. At these festive meals, Columbus was amazed by the thick strands of pearls the women wore. The weather was pleasant, and he marveled at the countryside filled with native farmers tending orchards and grapevines. Columbus thought he must be in the Garden of Eden. He called this country Los Jardines, or The Gardens. He thought Spain would reap great *profit* from this country. Even though he thought this land was part of Asia, however, he also wondered where the spice trees, precious stones, and the great cities of gold were.

One of the first Europeans to see South America was the Portuguese explorer Pedro Álvares Cabral (inset). In 1500, during a voyage around the southern tip of Africa, Cabral was blown far off course to the west. He spotted land, which he claimed for Portugal; this turned out to be the coast of Brazil. The Cantino map from 1502 is one of the earliest that shows the continent.

Because of Columbus, every man in Europe dreamed of going to the New World to gain fame and fortune. Alonso de Ojeda was such a man. He was an officer on Columbus's third voyage. A year after this voyage, he sailed from Spain with Amerigo Vespucci, a Venetian merchant. They followed

Columbus's map and set off to the same area he had visited. After 25 days, they reached the South American
coast. From here, Ojeda and Vespucci separated. Ojeda
sailed west, and Vespucci sailed south down the coast.

Ojeda was looking mainly for pearls. He first landed
on Trinidad, the island Columbus had discovered off the
coast of present-day Venezuela. There, Ojeda fought with
some Caribs, a native tribe that lived on many of the
islands of the Caribbean. These Caribs may have been
some of the same natives who shot arrows at Columbus's
dancing crew.

Ojeda explored the northern coast of South America
and inland to Lake Maracaibo, where the natives lived in
huts on stilts. These villages over the water reminded him
of houses along the canals of Venice, Italy. He named the
area "Venezuela," or "little Venice." He explored as far as
Columbia before returning to the island of Hispaniola.
Columbus had founded one of the first Spanish colonies
on Hispaniola. It was the home port for much of the early
Spanish exploration of the New World. Today, the island
is divided into two countries: Haiti and the Dominican
Republic. Ojeda sailed back to Spain in 1500 with a cargo
of pearls, brazilwood (used for making dyes), and natives
to be sold as slaves.

While Ojeda was looking for treasure, Vespucci was

going in the opposite direction. He was searching for a route to India. The continents of North and South America were completely unknown to Europeans at that time, and Vespucci was using a very old map. The map showed a long, narrow piece of Asia that stuck far out into the ocean. Vespucci thought that if he could find a way around this *peninsula*, he would be in Asia. Because Vespucci was a merchant, he knew great wealth was to be had from trading in spices. Like Columbus, he wanted to be the first man to find a western route to Asia. He was looking for a *strait*, or passageway, that would allow him to get around these newly discovered "islands." He had no idea that a huge continent, not an island, stood in his way.

On June 27, 1499, Vespucci became the first European to see the coast of Brazil. He was also the first to explore the mighty Amazon River. His two ships sailed a short distance up the Amazon. He then set out in a smaller boat, rowing upstream for about 75 miles. He and his men marveled at the exotic beauty of the lush rainforest and the colorful parrots, but they saw no people or settlements.

Vespucci then realized the same thing that Columbus had. A river this size could never come from an island. He also realized that the old map he was using was wrong. He sailed farther down the Brazilian coast of South America. He was still trying to sail around this new land and reach

Amerigo Vespucci explored the coast of South America for both Spain and Portugal. Unlike Columbus, Vespucci understood that North and South America were continents that had previously been unknown to Europeans. Vespucci also wrote many letters about the places he visited and the people he met during his expeditions. In 1507, German mapmaker Martin Waldseemüller applied Vespucci's first name to the new continent: America.

AMERICVS VESPVCCI

Asia when he came upon a strong current that he could not sail against. He turned back up the coast of South America and made his way back to Trinidad. He sailed into Lake Maracaibo, thinking he had found the strait. When he hit the other shore, he was very disappointed. He renamed the lake Deceitful Gulf. By this point, his ships were now riddled with *shipworms*. He had to return to Hispaniola, where he rejoined Ojeda.

After Vespucci's return to Spain, he said he and the other explorers had not found Asia. Vespucci declared he had actually discovered a new continent that lay between Europe and Asia. This was important for explorers to understand.

Amerigo Vespucci made another voyage to Brazil from 1501 to 1504, this time for Portugal instead of Spain. He was still trying to find the route to Asia. Although he did not succeed, Vespucci did find a river which he named Rio de Janeiro.

During his own time, people believed that Amerigo Vespucci had discovered these new continents before Columbus. They gave his first name to them—North and South America. Actually, Vespucci did not reach South America until after Columbus. By the time people realized the truth, however, it was too late to change the name of the continents. If they had realized this earlier, today the continents might be known as North and South Columbia.

Now that a new continent had been discovered, the King wanted a *colony* there. He sent Ojeda on a second voyage in 1502. Ojeda established the first Spanish colony on the north coast of South America. However, the colony was a failure and was soon abandoned. Ojeda was arrested by his partners for cheating them and for brutalizing the natives. He was found guilty, but his sentence was overturned, and Ojeda returned to Spain. This happened to many of the *conquistadors*. The same reckless bravery that made them great discoverers sometimes got them into trouble with the King and his governors.

In 1508, Ojeda gathered a force of 220 Spaniards, including a soldier named Francisco Pizarro, for a third voyage. He tried to establish his colony on the site where Colombia's main port, Cartagena, now stands. He again got into a fight with the local people. The group's navigator was killed by a poisoned arrow, and Ojeda himself was badly wounded.

The colony then faced starvation, and Ojeda sailed to the port of Santo Domingo on Hispaniola to get supplies. While he was gone, Pizarro and Vasco Núñez de Balboa moved the colony to Panama.

On his way to Santo Domingo, Ojeda was shipwrecked on the island of Cuba. He made a desperate trek along Cuba's southern coast and a miraculous journey by sea to Jamaica. He finally reached Santo Domingo, but never made it back to his colony. Ojeda lived the rest of his life in poverty. Some say he joined a monastery in Santo Domingo—a very different life from that of a conquistador.

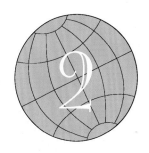

Balboa's March to the Pacific

THE MOST IMPORTANT discovery of the 15th century was Columbus's finding South America. The second most important was Vasco Núñez de Balboa's discovery of the Pacific Ocean. This proved for certain that the lands explored by the conquistadors were not part of Asia but a new world, just as Vespucci had claimed.

Balboa was a brave soldier and a good leader. When he came to South America, he met Francisco Pizarro. The two adventurers became friends. Together they rescued a starving settlement that Alonso de Ojeda had started on the north coast of South America. They moved the settlement to the coast of Panama and named it Santa Maria de

Vasco Núñez de Balboa

Vasco Núñez de Balboa was born in Jerez in the Extremadura region of Spain in 1475. The smell of the sea and the songs of sailors filled Balboa's childhood. He left for the New World when he was 26.

Balboa sailed to Hispaniola, the main Spanish colony in the New World. He became a farmer, but soon ran out of money. To escape bill collectors, he hid on a ship in an empty wine barrel with his dog. Once at sea, Balboa leaped out of the barrel and begged to be allowed to work as a sailor. The ship was bringing supplies to a starving settlement that had been founded by Alonso de Ojeda. When they arrived at the settlement, Balboa met Francisco Pizarro and helped him move the colony to a better site on the coast of Panama.

In Panama, Balboa made friends with the local chief, who told him about a very rich people across the sea to the south. Balboa wanted to find this sea and this land of gold. With a small force of about 100 soldiers, Balboa cut his way through miles of thick forest. He fought alligators, giant snakes, and attacks by hostile tribes. On September 29, 1513, he waded into the surf of a huge new ocean never before seen by Europeans. With his sword raised, he named it the South Sea and claimed it for the King and Queen of Spain.

Jealous rivals eventually had Balboa arrested and executed in 1519.

la Antigua. It was the first permanent European settlement on the American mainland. The king of Spain placed Balboa in charge of the settlement and ordered him to make the area safe for settlers and to send back any gold he found. Balboa proved to be very good at both of these things.

Balboa, along with his dog Leoncillo, explored the coast around Santa Maria and formed friendships with the natives. He baptized two caciques and eventually married the daughter of one of them.

One day, Balboa was weighing a gift of gold at the house of Comogre, one of the caciques. The chief's son knocked over the scales, spilling the gold onto the ground. Balboa was angry at first. But then, the chief's son pointed to the south and said that much more gold could be found across the sea. He told Balboa that with 1,000 soldiers he could conquer that rich land. Balboa decided to find this sea and the land of gold.

With a small force of about

Balboa and the other conquistadors used their large war dogs to attack unfriendly natives. It is said that Leoncillo, Balboa's dog, would enter a village and put his mouth gently around a man's arm and lead him back to Balboa's camp. He would not harm the man as long as he followed. But if the man resisted, Leoncillo would tear him apart with his strong jaws.

a hundred men, Balboa began cutting his way through the jungles of Panama. Again, he took his dog Leoncillo. They crossed rivers teeming with crocodiles and waded through swamps with huge snakes. They carried their clothes on their heads to keep them from rotting in the foul water. The forest was so thick that they sometimes did not see the sun for days.

Balboa's expedition was getting close to the mountains that run down the center of Panama, the Serranías de Maje. All of a sudden, a fierce cacique named Torecha appeared with an army of warriors. Torecha ordered the Spanish to turn back, but Balboa was not going to stop now. The Spaniards attacked Torecha's warriors and killed 600 of them, including Torecha.

Several days later, Balboa climbed to the top of a mountain peak and saw some water in the distance. He said a prayer and continued to make his way towards the water. When he got there, he realized this was no lake or sea but a vast ocean bigger than any he had ever seen before. It was less than 100 miles from the Atlantic. Balboa drew his sword and marched into the waves. He claimed the sea and the countries bordering it for the King. However, this was not of interest to Balboa. He was looking for the cities of gold to the south.

Balboa returned to Antigua and built four ships. His

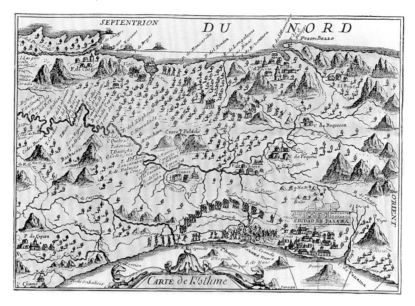

Panama, shown in a colored woodcut from a Spanish book about the New World, was an untamed, dangerous land when Vasco Núñez de Balboa arrived there in the early 16th century. Balboa's discovery of the South Sea was one of the most important finds since Columbus had landed in the New World.

shipbuilders made them in pieces, then Balboa had native *laborers* carry the pieces to the opposite shore on the Pacific. Many natives died making this difficult trip. The boats were eventually assembled, and Balboa sailed out into the Pacific. The winds were blowing in the wrong direction, however, and forced him back to shore. Balboa never made it to the west coast of South America or Peru. He never saw the cities of gold he had tried so hard to find and was so close to actually discovering.

Not long after that, Balboa got into trouble with the new governor the king had sent to Central America, a man named Pedro Arias de Avila. Neither man trusted the other. One day, Arias sent Pizarro to arrest Balboa on a made-up charge of **treason** and mistreating the natives. In a fixed trial, Balboa was found guilty. He was taken to the public square, where his fellow explorer Pizarro cut off his head.

When the news of Balboa's discovery reached Spain, the King, now more than ever, wanted to find a way for ships to get from Europe to the new ocean. The Spanish needed a western route to Asia and the profitable spice route. The Portuguese had already laid claim to the eastern route to India by sailing around the southern tip of Africa. Now the Spanish saw there might be a western route to the rich Spice Islands. They just needed to find a way through the continent that stood in the way.

A number of Spanish explorers sailed up and down the coast of South America, looking for a water passage through the continent. The Spaniards believed that Asia was located to the west across the Pacific Ocean, and they were right. However, they also though it was close—perhaps just a few days' sail away. This belief was incorrect, as an explorer named Ferdinand Magellan proved.

Ferdinand Magellan had been a captain in the Portuguese navy. He had sailed to India and the Spice Islands by following the eastward route—south around Africa, then east across the Indian Ocean. However, the

Ferdinand Magellan had been born into a noble family and had an important job at the royal court of the queen of Portugal. In 1505, when he was 26 years old, he gave up his position to join Portugal's navy. He sailed with a large fleet of warships commanded by Francisco de Almeida to the Indian Ocean, where Portugal wanted to establish its trading posts. The fleet's intention was to destroy the ships of Arab traders who competed with the Portuguese. Magellan spent seven years as a ship's captain in the East.

king of Portugal had become unhappy with Magellan, and would not allow him to make any more voyages for Portugal.

Undaunted, Magellan went to Portugal's rival, Spain. He told King Charles V of Spain about his plan to reach India and the Spice Islands by sailing west across the Atlantic. After they had talked about the plan for a long time, the King finally gave Magellan the ships he needed. He sailed out of port in 1519 with 5 Spanish ships and about 280 sailors.

They reached the Brazilian coast in 1520 and sailed south. They explored every cove and inlet for the

Ferdinand Magellan

Twenty-seven years after Columbus's first voyage, Ferdinand Magellan set out from Spain on what would be one of the greatest ocean voyages during the Age of Exploration.

Magellan was born in Portugal to a noble family in 1480. In 1505, he sailed with the Portuguese navy around the tip of Africa and to the Spice Islands. He served in the Indian Ocean for the next seven years. As a result, he was very familiar with Portugal's eastern trading routes to Asia. He also fought with Portugal's army in Morocco.

When Magellan returned to Portugal, he was falsely accused of crimes. Although he proved himself innocent, the Portuguese king still refused to allow him to sail under the Portuguese flag.

Magellan then moved to Spain, where he convinced the king that he could find a western route to the Spice Islands. His fleet of five ships left Spain in September of 1519. Magellan explored the coast of South America for several months until he found a route through the continent to the Pacific Ocean.

Magellan did not survive the voyage. However, his determination and firm leadership made the first voyage around the world possible. He did more than any other man to show the Spanish how big the lands of the New World were. He also extended these lands by leading the way to the Philippines, which would eventually come under Spanish rule.

passageway to the South Sea, as the Pacific Ocean was then called. After six months of searching the coastline, the cold winter weather forced them to take shelter in a bay. During the hard winter, Magellan had to cut food *rations* to the crew. On April

The crew on Magellan's voyage was made up of sailors from many different nations, including Italy, France, Africa, Greece, and Malaysia, as well as Spain and Portugal.

1, the hungry men rebelled in a *mutiny* on three of the five ships. However, Magellan and the men who remained loyal to him soon recaptured the ships and punished the leaders of the mutiny.

While they spent seven long months at anchor waiting for the weather to improve, Magellan visited the natives of the area. He gave them the nickname "Patagones," or "big feet," because of the large, fur-covered *moccasins* they wore. Later, this country south of Brazil was called Patagonia.

Once summer arrived, Magellan and his men were able to continued their voyage. After sailing for three days, they came to what looked like another bay. Magellan spent five weeks making his way through rocks, reefs, and glaciers and fighting the strong winds. One ship *deserted* the voyage during the difficult passage without

This drawing from a 16th-century German book about Magellan's voyage shows the explorer receiving a hostile reception from the natives of South America.

informing Magellan. Magellan searched for the missing ship. When he could not find it, he refused to turn back. He vowed that, "if they had to eat the leather on the yards [part of the ship's mast], he would still go on."

On November 28, 1520, the three surviving ships sailed into the calm waters of a strange, new ocean. The wind was unusually calm, and Magellan named the new sea El Mar Pacifico, or Peaceful Sea. He thought Asia must be very close and within his grasp.

Magellan and his three ships sailed for 98 days across the vast Pacific, seeing only two small *isles* the whole time. They were running out of food again. Magellan had to live up to the words of his earlier vow not to turn back. He wrote in his ship's log, "We ate biscuit, but in truth it was biscuit no longer but a powder of worms . . . we used sawdust for food and rats were such a delicacy that we paid half a ducat apiece for them." A disease called *scurvy* broke out, and some of the crew died.

On March 6, 1521, land was finally sighted. They sailed on to a group of islands known as the Philippine Islands. There, the crew regained their strength on fruits and vegeta-

> **Scurvy is a disease that sailors often get from not eating enough vitamin C—found in citrus fruits. It causes weakness, inflamed gums, loose teeth, and swollen joints.**

A colored woodcut of the *Victoria*, the only one of Magellan's ships to return to Spain. It arrived in 1522, three years after his fleet of five ships had set out. Of the 275 men who set out with Magellan, only 18 survived the journey around the world.

bles. These islands were not known to Europeans at the time, but were visited by Chinese traders. Magellan learned that the Spice Islands were due south of the Philippines.

Columbus had dreamed of finding a shortcut to the Indies and the rich spice trade of Asia, and now Magellan had done it. He had found the strait through South America to the Pacific, sailed across the unknown ocean, and reached the Spice Islands by sailing west. This was the same area the Portuguese had explored by sailing east. The world was indeed round.

However, the life of an explorer was always dangerous. Soon after this, Magellan was killed in a battle with some warring natives. Juan Sebastian de Elcano, the captain of one of the remaining ships, continued Magellan's voyage. He kept sailing west through the Indian Ocean and around the horn of Africa. In September 1522, he arrived in Seville, Spain, with one ship and a handful of men. Elcano became the first to sail completely around the globe. It had taken him almost three years to complete this amazing journey.

> **The Spice Islands were also known as the Moluccas. They were the main source of nutmeg, mace, and cloves. Today, they are part of Indonesia.**

Francisco Pizarro was ruthless, fearless, cruel, and smart, as he proved by taking on the vast Inca empire. The Incas had the most highly developed civilization in South America. It was centered around their cities on the western coast of the continent.

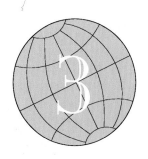

The Conquest of Peru

WHEN FRANCISCO PIZARRO came to the New World at the age of 27, he was just a poor soldier. But he soon proved himself to be brave and cunning. He was also ruthless, greedy, and cruel. He was the man who executed Balboa after marching alongside him to discover the Pacific Ocean. During his exploits with Balboa in Panama, he heard many stories of a land of gold located to the south in Peru. Also during this time, Hernán Cortés's conquest of Mexico was the talk of Spain and the New World. Pizarro thought Peru might be an even richer prize. No matter what it took, Pizarro was determined to get his share of the gold and glory. He was going to conquer Peru.

In 1524, Pizarro formed a partnership with another adventurer, Diego de Almagro. Their goal was to find and conquer the great empire of Peru. Pizarro and Almagro spent the next eight years and three voyages together exploring the west coast of South America—climbing mountains, crossing deserts, fighting natives, and suffering disease and starvation.

Their first expedition, into Ecuador and Colombia in 1524, was a failure. Although they did gain some gold, they ran out of food and had to return to the Spanish colony in Panama. In 1526, Pizarro and Almagro set out again from Panama, sailing down the west coast of South America. There he came to a port with stone buildings and well-kept

Pizarro formed a partnership with Diego de Almagro, another Spanish soldier. They intended to work together to conquer the Incas. However, disagreements between the two conquistadors eventually erupted into a fight that would cost both men their lives.

fields. These stone buildings were different from any he had seen in the rest of the New World. To Pizarro, this meant that he was nearing a great civilization and the gold cities he was seeking. The inhabitants, however, were hostile, and Pizarro retreated to a safe island off the coast. He stayed on the island while Almagro returned to Panama for more supplies and men. The new governor of Panama refused to send more supplies. Instead, he sent a ship to bring the men back. When the governor's ship arrived, Pizarro and his men were starving and in rags. But Pizarro still wanted to continue looking for the gold. He drew a line on the ground with his sword. He pointed at the far side of the line, toward the south, saying, "There lies Peru with its riches." He then pointed at the near side and said, "And here, Panama and its poverty. For my part, I go south." Thirteen men stepped over the line and stayed with Pizarro. The rest sailed back to Panama.

Pizarro suffered seven more months of starvation and heavy rains before Almagro managed to bring food and supplies. They then sailed south and stopped at the Incan port of Tumbes. There they met an Incan nobleman. He was dressed in richly woven cloth, gold jewelry, and feathers. The nobleman showed them temples covered in gold and precious jewels. They followed a stone road leading up into the Andes. This road led to the capital of the Incan empire.

The Spanish Exploration of South America

Pizarro was now certain that this was the empire of gold he was seeking, but he did not have enough soldiers to complete his conquest. Pizarro decided that instead of going to the governor, who had not wanted to help before, he would go directly to the king of Spain and ask for the ships and troops he needed.

For a year Pizarro tried to convince the king that he should be governor of the country of Peru. The king finally agreed. Almagro was to be governor of the city of Tumbes. Pizarro also got his brothers, Martin, Gonzalo, Juan, Pedro, and Hernando, to come with him on the expedition. Almagro was angry at his smaller share and his lesser position, but for the moment he agreed that Pizarro would lead the expedition. Almagro would follow with reinforcements.

In 1530, Pizarro, his brothers, 180 additional men, and their horses sailed out from Panama to conquer Peru. Pizarro returned to Tumbes and found it in ruins. He learned of a civil war between two brothers, Atahuallpa and Huascar, for the throne of the Incan Empire. Pizarro received a messenger from Huascar, the rightful heir, asking for his aid. Pizarro pledged to help him gain the throne. Actually, he was using the rivalry between Atahuallpa and his brother to further his own conquest plans. He learned that Atahuallpa's army was camped at the city of Cajamarca.

Civil War Divides the Incan Empire

The Inca empire was the largest native civilization in South America in the 16th century. It stretched from the west coast to the jungles of the Amazon River and from Peru to Chile. This vast empire was tied together with one of the world's best road systems. The roads connected cities built of cut stone, fortresses, temples, and irrigated farms.

However, when Pizarro and the Spaniards arrived in South America, the empire was in disarray. The emperor Huayna Capac had died of smallpox in 1527. Smallpox was a disease that had been brought by people from Europe. Natives Americans had no resistance to the disease, and it killed millions of natives in both North and South America.

Some say that Huayna Capac died so quickly that he did not have time to appoint a new emperor. Others say that he had intended to divide the empire between Atahuallpa and his brother, Huascar. In any case, Atahuallpa attacked Huascar's army in a bloody battle near the capital city of Cuzco. He destroyed Huascar's forces, then massacred Huascar and his family, so there would be no question about who was the rightful ruler.

After his victory, the emperor Atahuallpa made his headquarters in the city of Cajamarca. He was a supreme emperor with a battle-tested army of over 40,000 soldiers.

Francisco Pizarro

Francisco Pizarro, conqueror of Peru, was born in 1475 in the town of Trujillo. Like many of his fellow conquistadors, he was from the region of Spain called Extremadura. As a child, he lived with his grandmother and herded pigs. He never went to school or learned to read or write. He did not have much of a future in Spain, so he traveled to the New World to make his fortune in 1502.

Pizarro sailed with Alonso de Ojeda to start a colony on the north coast of South America. A few years later, he marched with Balboa across Panama to discover the Pacific Ocean in 1513. In his early adventures, Pizarro proved himself to be brave, but also ruthless and cunning, willing to do whatever was necessary to get what he wanted. And what he wanted more than anything else was gold. He had heard many stories about cities of gold located to the south in Peru. In order to get the ships and men he needed to find the gold of the Inca empire, he formed a partnership with Diego de Almagro.

Pizarro's first attempt to invade South America, in 1526, failed. He set out again in 1530. This time, his small army succeeded in subjugating the Inca empire.

Pizarro would only enjoy his wealth for a few years. Almagro and Pizarro fought over the Inca riches. Pizarro defeated Almagro, but then was killed in his own palace by Almagro supporters in 1541.

Pizarro began his march into the Andes. With a small force of 62 cavalry and 106 *infantry* they climbed the cold peaks of the Andes. Pizarro sent Hernando de Soto to scout out what lay ahead. De Soto returned in five days with a messenger from Atahuallpa. The messenger gave Pizarro bracelets of gold and a pair of gold shoes to wear so the Incan emperor could recognize him.

The route up the mountains was cold, difficult, and dangerous. The Incas could have stopped the Spaniards at any time, but Atahuallpa believed such a small force was no threat to his mighty army. He thought it was actually coming to surrender to him.

To reach the important cities of the Incas, Spanish soldiers had to march across the Andes, a tall chain of mountains that stretches across the western coast of South America. Because of the high altitudes, many of the Spanish soldiers became sick and weak. They would have been vulnerable had the Incas decided to attack, especially since there were fewer than 200 Spanish soldiers. However, the Incas allowed the Spaniards to proceed.

After 45 day of hard climbing, Pizarro led his men in full battle dress toward Cajamarca. As the men marched toward the city, they were terrified by the huge army camped in a city of tents surrounding Cajamarca. Pizarro was determined to show no fear, however, and boldly marched into the deserted city.

Pizarro sent de Soto to invite Atahuallpa to visit him in the city. Then he hid his men in buildings around the town square. Atahuallpa entered the city on a gold throne carried by nobles and accompanied by 5,000 unarmed warriors. Atahuallpa stopped in the center of the square and asked where the strangers were. He was told that they were hiding in fear. Although this was supposed to be a trick, many of the Spanish soldiers were, in fact, "shivering from fright," according to Pedro Pizarro. Pizarro then gave the signal. Cannons, *harquebusiers*, and crossbows fired. Horses charged. The infantry rushed out of the buildings and cut down the defenseless Incas.

Pizarro's small force slaughtered several thousand Inca warriors without losing a single man. In fact, Pizarro had to rescue Atahuallpa from the blood-crazed Spanish soldiers. Pizarro had now accomplished his simple plan—to capture the emperor alive and thereby rule the empire. This was exactly how Cortés had conquered the Aztecs in Mexico during the 1520s.

When the Spaniards attacked the Incas in Cajamarca, Pizarro fought his way through Atahuallpa's guard and seized the Inca ruler from his litter. Once the Incas saw their leader caught, they retreated from the battlefield. The Spaniards were able to rout the much larger force, slaughtering thousands of Incas.

In exchange for his freedom, Atahuallpa offered to fill a room 17 feet by 22 feet with gold to a height of 9 feet. Pizarro quickly agreed. When this fantastic treasure was delivered, however, Pizarro put Atahuallpa on trial for crimes against Christianity. The judges found the emperor guilty and had him executed in 1533. Later that year, the Spanish seized the capital Cuzco and stripped the Incan

After the Incas paid a huge ransom of gold and silver to free their emperor, Pizarro put Atahuallpa on trial. Atahuallpa was sentenced to be burned at the stake. However, he asked to be converted to Christianity so he could be strangled instead. This was a less painful death and would spare his soul in the afterlife. Pizarro granted his wish.

empire of its riches with little opposition. Pizarro then built his capital in Lima.

Pizarro controlled the Incas, but he was soon facing a new enemy—his former partner Diego de Almagro. Almagro was still angry with Pizarro for not giving him his fair share. A civil war broke out between the supporters of the two Spanish leaders. In 1538 Almagro was defeated at the battle of Salinas by Hernando Pizarro, Francisco's brother. Almagro was taken prisoner, then executed by Pizarro.

But that was not the end of the war. Three years later, 20 Almagro supporters entered Pizarro's palace. They attacked and killed the great conquistador.

The Search for Cinnamon and El Dorado

CINNAMON IS A COMMON spice today. In the time of the conquistadors, however, it was valued as much as gold. The only place to get it was Asia, and Portugal controlled the route to that country.

Gonzalo Pizarro, the brother of Francisco Pizarro, had heard stories from the natives of South America that forests of cinnamon trees grew on the other side of the Andes Mountains. He had also heard of a very rich land around Lake El Dorado. According to the legend, gold was so plentiful in El Dorado that every day the king of the region covered his body with gold dust, which he washed off at sunset. If he could find either this land of spices or of gold, Gonzalo

45

> **Cinnamon comes from the bark of a tree. The best cinnamon is grown in Sri Lanka, a large island off the southern coast of India.**

would gain treasure even greater than that gained by his brother from the Incas.

When Gonzalo decided to search for the cinnamon trees, he *recruited* 200 foot soldiers, 100 cavalry soldiers with horses, and 4,000 Indians to serve as guides and laborers. The party also took along 4,000 pigs and a herd of llamas to use as food, as well as hundreds of war dogs.

A man named Francisco de Orellana was eager to join Gonzalo in his quest for gold and cinnamon. Orellana was a relative of the Pizarros. He was also the governor of Guayquil, a city on the coast of Peru. Orellana resigned his government office. With about 30 men, he hurried to join Gonzalo's adventure. By the time he reached Quito, however, Pizarro's large expedition had already left. Orellana had to catch up with them as best he could.

As Pizarro climbed the steep mountains, many Indians died of the cold. To get information on where the cinnamon trees were located, Gonzalo tortured and burned many of the local natives. The natives did not know where the great groves of cinnamon trees lay, but they did tell Pizarro something he wanted to hear—lands rich in gold and jewels lay farther to the east, always farther to the east.

Francisco de Orellana

Francisco de Orellana was born in Trujillo, Spain in 1511. He was from the same town as Francisco Pizarro. In fact, Pizarro was one of his relatives. Not much is known about his early life, but he left for the New World when he was only 16, and served with Pizarro in the conquest of Peru. He fought against the Incas at Lima and at Cuzco. In one battle, he lost an eye. After Peru was conquered, he was awarded a large farm in Ecuador.

Orellana rushed to Pizarro's defense when the civil war with Diego de Almagro broke out. When Pizarro's side won, Orellana was rewarded with the position of lieutenant-governor of the coastal town of Guayaquil. Orellana could not resist a good adventure, however. In 1542 he resigned his position and joined Gonzalo Pizarro on a quest to look for the gold of El Dorado in the forests on the east side of the Andes. This expedition did not go well. They soon found themselves starving in the jungles surrounding the Amazon River. While looking for food, Orellana became the first European to travel the entire length of the Amazon—an amazing journey of over 5000 miles.

Orellana's luck did not continue, however. Three years later, he left Spain on a voyage to colonize the Amazon region. He only made it a short way into the mouth of the Amazon River when his ship was wrecked. Orellana died of fever on an island in the Amazon River in November 1546.

The reason we know so much about this trip is that a priest, Carvajal, who went with Orellana, wrote an account of their voyage. Priests often traveled with the conquistadors to preach to the men and convert the natives to Christianity. They did a great service to later generations in writing these eyewitness histories.

After Orellana caught up with Pizarro, a scouting party was sent ahead. Though they found no evidence of El Dorado, they did discover a great river. This was the Coca, which eventually flows into the Amazon. Pizarro reached the Coca River in November 1541, seven months after leaving Quito. Most of the Indians were dead, and the pigs and llamas had all been eaten. The Spaniards were nearly starving, but Pizarro continued, spurred on by the golden promise of El Dorado.

To make traveling along the river easier, Gonzalo ordered Orellana to build a boat to carry the baggage and the sick. Orellana built a small 20-foot boat and volunteered to go downstream to look for food. Orellana and his men planned to sail down river no more than a few days and then return.

When Orellana did not return, Gonzalo had no choice but to turn back. He made his way with great difficulty back to Quito with less than half the men he had started out with

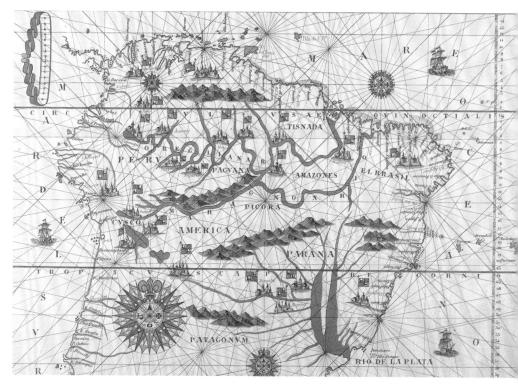

This detail from a Spanish map of South America made in 1582 shows the route of the Amazon River.

18 months before. Pizarro was angry that Orellana never returned. When he got back to Quito, he wrote to the King accusing Orellana of desertion.

Meanwhile, the rapid current had quickly carried Orellana's boat down river. They didn't encounter any villages for eight days. They had nothing to eat "but leather, belts, and soles of shoes with certain herbs." On the eighth day, they heard drums in the distance. The next day, they saw a village and rushed ashore. Fortunately, the natives were friendly and there was plenty of food.

Orellana and his sailors realized that it would take many days to return upstream against the fast-flowing current to rejoin Pizarro. He decided to continue down the river. He soon reached the main branch of the Amazon. Here they stopped at a village for a month and built a bigger boat.

Sailing down the Amazon in their larger boat, they encountered many hostile tribes. Carvajal, a member of the expedition, later wrote that in one battle, the Indians "began to attack us and fight like ravenous dogs." The sailors lost some men to poisonous arrows, but the natives were no match for the crossbows and guns of the Spanish.

On June 3, they saw the wide mouth of a river with dark waters flowing into the Amazon. These black waters did not mix with the brown waters of the Amazon for many miles. Orellana named this river Rio Negro, "Black River," and it still has that name today.

Two days after passing the Rio Negro, Orellana and his men met some Indians who claimed to belong to a nation ruled by women. Soon after this, they were attacked by natives who were led by women archers. Carvajal called these women "Amazons" after the mythical Greek women who were the warriors of Scythia. Carvajal describes these women as very tall and light-skinned. He says they fought in front of the men with bows and arrows and shot anyone who ran away from the battle. This story of the Amazons caused quite a stir in Europe. This is how the Amazon River got its name.

After overcoming poison arrows and women warriors, Orellana finally sailed into a peaceful part of the river. At this place, the river was very wide and the land very flat. The sailors could feel the movement of the ocean tide beneath the boat. Islands appeared in the middle of the ever-widening river, and they soon lost sight of the shore. They still didn't have much food and had to resort to raiding villages to get something to eat. They also had to stop and repair the boats. The skillful seamen made sails from blankets and rigged them with vines.

Orellana sailed out of the mouth of the Amazon on August 26, 1542. Carvajal says the river was over 150 miles wide as it flowed into the Atlantic. It was like two oceans meeting. While Orellana was an excellent sailor, he did not want to sail into the open ocean with a boat made for the river. He hugged the coast of Guiana and reached the port of Cubagua off the coast of Venezuela. Orellana and his brave crew had spent eight months on the world's mightiest river, traveling over 5,000 miles to its mouth—truly an incredible journey!

This statue of Pedro de Valdivia watches over the streets of Valparaíso, Chile's main seaport. In 1540 Valdivia led a Spanish expedition to conquer the native Araucania civilization. He established several cities along the southwestern coast of South America.

The Conquest of Chile

THE SHAPE OF CHILE has been compared to the blade of a sword—long and narrow. But it is like a sword in another way as well. For the Spanish, it was one of the bloodiest and most difficult countries of South America to conquer.

Pedro de Valdivia was a conquistador who served under Francisco Pizarro in the conquest of Peru. Valdivia also sided with Pizarro in his civil war with Almagro. The victorious Pizarro rewarded Valdivia by giving him the governorship of Chile. But there were already people and tribes living in Chile. How could Pizarro give away another people's land? The conquistadors thought it was their right to claim the lands for the King. They also thought it was their duty to convert the natives to Christianity. They believed that in doing this they were helping the natives.

In 1540, Valdivia set out with a small force of 150 Spaniards and 1,000 Indians to claim Chile for Spain. To get there, Valdivia had to climb the cold, snowy Andes Mountains and cross the bone-dry Atacama Desert. But once he arrived, it was different. All the other countries the Spanish had conquered were hot and rainy. Chile had a mild climate that was more like what they were used to in Europe.

The Atacama Desert is the world's driest area. The desert town of Calama recorded a 400-year drought that finally ended in 1971.

Marching south, Valdivia and his Spanish soldiers came upon beautiful and fertile valleys. In one of these, many almond trees bloomed. Valdivia named it Valparaíso, or Valley of Paradise. Today, Valparaíso is Chile's main seaport.

Going farther south, Valdivia came to the Maile River. In a valley along the Maile, Valdivia founded the city of Santiago on a rock that formed a natural fortress. Today, this city is Chile's capital.

Now, the Spanish were in the territory of the Araucanians. They were a fierce and brave people and very much against the Spanish settling in their country. They

This Native American painting on cloth shows Spanish priests holding a religious ceremony with converted Indians. One of the goals of conquistadors in the New World was to convert the native people they met to Christianity.

took every opportunity to starve out the Spaniards. Valdivia had to constantly guard his city and crops from Araucanian raids. One day, when he was away getting supplies from Peru, the Araucanians attacked. Only 50 Spaniards had been left to defend the town. Valdivia's able lieutenant, Alonso de Monroy, led the city's defense. Ines Suarez, the only Spanish woman in the colony, was one of the bravest defenders. Dressed in a suit of armor, she led a cavalry charge against the attackers. The Spanish managed to drive off the Araucanians, but not before the aggressive native warriors set fire to the city and burned it to the ground. The Araucanians were one of the few native peoples to win battles against the Spanish, at least for a while.

Valdivia returned with supplies and reinforcements from Peru. He rebuilt and expanded his colony. Despite repeated attacks by the Araucanians, Valdivia pushed south towards the southern tip of South America. He founded the city of Concepción. It is now Chile's second largest city. Farther down the coast, he built seven Spanish outposts. He named the last and largest after himself, Valdivia, in 1552.

Meanwhile, the Araucanians did not give up their fight against the Spanish invasion of their homeland. They rallied behind the leadership of a chief named Lautaro. Lautaro had once been a slave to Valdivia, but escaped. As Valdivia was returning from his explorations, Lautaro and his army were waiting. The fierce Araucanian warriors attacked in overwhelming numbers. All the Spanish were killed. Valdivia was captured and tortured to death. Some accounts of the event say they poured molten gold down Valdivia's throat. This may have been done to show their disgust for the Spanish thirst for gold, or as revenge for the many native South Americans tortured and killed by the Spaniards. The war between the Spanish and the Araucanians would last for another 250 years.

Valdivia and the other conquistadors were young, brave men; sometimes they could be ruthless and cruel. But it was largely through their efforts that a new continent was opened up for the joining of two great cultures. The influence of the Spanish conquistadors and explorers has remained strong in South America into the 21st century.

Chronology

1492 On October 12, Christopher Columbus spots land in the Atlantic Ocean (Watlings Islands in the Bahamas); on December 6, Columbus discovers Hispaniola (the island that today is the countries of Haiti and the Dominican Republic).

1498 On May 30, Columbus sets out on his third voyage, landing in South America on August 2.

1499 Alonso de Ojeda and Amerigo Vespucci discover Venezuela.

1506 Columbus dies in Spain.

1513 Vasco Núñez de Balboa leads a Spanish force across the isthmus of Panama and discovers the Pacific Ocean, which he calls the South Sea.

1516 Charles I becomes king of Spain.

1520 Ferdinand Magellan, leading a Spanish expedition, discovers the strait through South America that is eventually named after him; King Charles I is crowned Holy Roman Emperor Charles V.

1521 Hernán Cortés conquers Mexico City; Magellan is killed in the Philippines.

1522 The survivors of Magellan's expedition return to Spain aboard the *Victoria*.

Chronology

1523 Francisco Pizarro sails for Peru from Panama.

1528 Pizarro is given permission to conquer Peru by Charles V.

1532 Pizarro takes the Inca emperor Atahuallpa prisoner at Cajamarca in May; large ransom of gold is collected.

1533 Atahuallpa is executed by the Spaniards in July; Pizarro's forces capture Cuzco, the last stronghold of the Inca forces.

1537 Almagro and his supporters begin fighting with Pizarro.

1538 Almagro is defeated by an army commanded by Francisco Pizarro's brother, Hernando.

1540 Pedro de Valdivia leads an expedition into Chile.

1541 Pizarro is assassinated by followers of Almagro on July 26; Valdivia founds Santiago; Gonzalo Pizarro sets out on a search for cinnamon forests and the fabled country of El Dorado. In December, he is joined by Francisco de Orellana and his men.

1452 Orellana crosses South America from west to east via the Amazon River.

1553 Lautaro and the Araucanians massacre the Spanish at Tucapel.

1554 Valdivia is tortured and killed by angry Native Americans.

Glossary

cacique—a Native American chief.

colony—a group of people living in a new territory but who still have connections with their original country.

conquistadors—leaders in the Spanish conquest of America and Mexico in the late 16th century.

desert—to leave or abandon a military position without permission and without intending to return.

harquebusiers—a heavy, portable gun that was usually fired from a support.

infantry—soldiers trained to fight on foot.

isles—islands.

laborer—somebody who works at a job that requires physical strength and stamina.

log—the record of a ship's voyage, usually kept by the captain.

moccasins—a soft, heelless shoe made out of leather.

mutiny—an organized revolt of a naval crew against a superior officer.

peninsula—a portion of land connected to a larger body of land and almost completely surrounded by water.

Glossary

profit—the difference between what a good or service costs to produce and the selling price.

ration—an allowance of food for one day.

recruit—to enlist somebody in a military force.

scurvy—a disease caused by a lack of vitamin C.

shipworm—a wormlike sea creature that burrows into submerged wood, damaging it.

spice—aromatic plant substances, such as cinnamon, nutmeg, and ginger, used as flavorings for food. Spices were very valuable in Europe during the 15th and 16th centuries.

strait—a narrow passageway connecting two bodies of water.

treason—a crime in which a person attempts to betray his or her government.

Further Reading

DeAngelis, Gina. *Francisco Pizarro and the Conquest of the Inca.*
Philadelphia: Chelsea House, 2001.

Diamond, Jared. *Guns, Germs, and Steel.* New York: W. W. Norton &
Company, 1998.

Konstam, Angus. *Historical Atlas of Exploration, 1492–1600.* New York:
Checkmark Books, 2000.

Marcovitz, Hal. *Vasco Núñez de Balboa and the Discovery of the South
Sea.* Philadelphia: Chelsea House, 2002.

Smith, Anthony. *Explorers of the Amazon.* New York: Viking
Penguin, 1990.

White, David. *The First Voyage Around the World.* Philadelphia:
Mason Crest, 2003.

Internet Resources

The Inca civilization and Spanish invasion
http://www.incaconquest.com
http://www.pbs.org/opb/conquistadors/home.htm

Exploration of the South American coast
http://www.acs.ucalgary.ca/HIST/tutor/eurvoya/index.html

Index

Photo Credits

About the Author

Mark McKain is a writer and editor in Los Angeles, California. He has written documentaries for PBS and animation scripts for Disney, Fox, and Warner Brothers. His fiction and poetry have appeared in magazines in both the United States and Great Britain. As a child, he lived in Puerto Rico, Louisiana, and Texas, where he first encountered the history and romance of the Spanish conquistadors.